Ayah Bdeir

Published in the United States of America by Cherry Lake Publishing
Ann Arbor, Michigan
www.cherrylakepublishing.com

Reading Adviser: Marla Conn, MS, Ed, Literacy specialist, Read-Ability, Inc.
Book Designer: Jennifer Wahi
Illustrator: Jeff Bane

Photo Credits: ©Vlad G/Shutterstock, 5; ©Yulia Grigoryeva/Shutterstock, 7; ©Dmytro Zinkevych/Shutterstock, 9;
©Joi Ito/flickr, 11; ©PopTech/flickr, 13, 22; ©littleBits/Wikimedia/Creative Commons Attribution Share-Alike 2.0
Generic, 15; ©LightField Studios/Shutterstock, 17; ©TechCrunch/flickr/Photo by Paul Zimmerman/Getty Images for
TechCrunch/AOL, 19, 23; ©Ea26nyc/Wikimedia/Creative Commons Attribution Share-Alike 4.0 International, 21;
Jeff Bane, cover, 1, 6, 12, 18

Library of Congress Cataloging-in-Publication Data

Names: Sarantou, Katlin, author. | Bane, Jeff, 1957- illustrator.
Title: Ayah Bdeir / by Katlin Sarantou ; illustrated by Jeff Bane.
Description: Ann Arbor : Cherry Lake Publishing, [2019] | Series: My
   itty-bitty bio | Includes bibliographical references and index.
Identifiers: LCCN 2019004197| ISBN 9781534146983 (hardcover) | ISBN
   9781534148413 (pdf) | ISBN 9781534149847 (pbk.) | ISBN 9781534151277
   (hosted ebook)
Subjects: LCSH: Bdeir, Ayah, 1982- | Inventors--United
   States--Biography--Juvenile literature. | Businesspeople--United
   States--Biography--Juvenile literature. | Educational toys--Juvenile
   literature. | Electronic apparatus and appliances--Juvenile literature.
Classification: LCC T40.B34 S37 2019 | DDC 338.7/62139092--dc23
LC record available at https://lccn.loc.gov/2019004197

Printed in the United States of America
Corporate Graphics

About the author: Katlin Sarantou grew up in the cornfields of Ohio. She enjoys reading and dreaming of faraway places.

About the illustrator: Jeff Bane and his two business partners own a studio along the American River in Folsom, California, home of the 1849 Gold Rush. When Jeff's not sketching or illustrating for clients, he's either swimming or kayaking in the river to relax.

I was born in Montreal, Canada.

It was 1982.

Then my family moved.

I grew up in Lebanon.

My parents taught me and my sisters to love science.

They wanted us to be **engineers**.

What have your parents taught you?

I went to school in the United States.

I studied computers and science.

I started the company littleBits **Electronics**.

I wanted all kids to create.

Do you have any ideas for a company?

littleBits are electronic blocks.

You use the blocks to build.

Magnets snap the blocks into place.

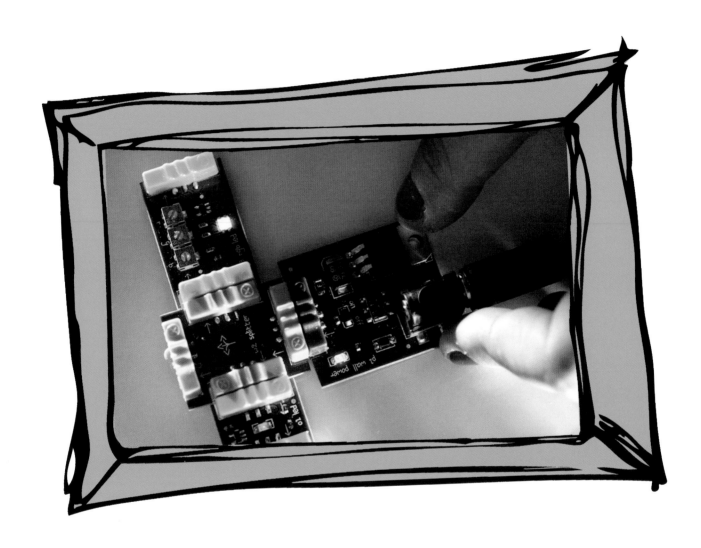

I made littleBits to be for boys and girls.

Everyone should be able to invent.

What is something you want to invent?

I have won many awards.

One is for being a woman leader.

19

I continue to **promote** easier **access** to technology.

I also do **workshops** to get girls interested in **STEAM**.

I inspire people to chase their dreams.

What would you like to ask me?

2011

1980

↑
Born
1982

2018

2080

glossary

access (AK-ses) having the chance to get something

electronics (ih-lek-TRAH-nikz) devices (such as televisions, radios, and computers) that work using many small electrical parts

engineers (en-juh-NEERZ) people who use science and math to design and build

magnets (MAG-nits) special metal pieces with two ends that can attract and pull each other

promote (pruh-MOTE) to make people aware of something or further its growth

STEAM (STEEM) stands for science, technology, engineering, art, and mathematics

workshops (WURK-shahps) meetings where people talk about and create something

index